50 PLUS YEARS
INVESTING IN
REAL ESTATE

For those who are interested in investing in flipping, building, or being a landlord with Real Estate.

I'm not giving professional advice for legal, tax, financial, structural, or architectural help.

If you need help in any of these, seek professional advice.

Published by:
Cheyenne Investments, LLC
Littleton, CO

Printed by Kindle Direct Publishing

First Edition

ISBN: 979-8-8732598-3-0

50 PLUS YEARS INVESTING IN REAL ESTATE

17 PROPERTIES

3 STATES

Flipping, Building, Renting

DUSTY HAGERTY

Dedication

To my wife Barb who has always supported me in
my Real Estate Investments since we met.
My mom who got me started.

Acknowledgments

Amy Terry, "my Realtor"

Since Chapter 11 Amy has done all my
Real Estate transactions.

Amy Terry—8Z Real Estate
303-882-3954
amyterry@8Z.com

Brandy who works in the photo lab at
Englewood Camera. englewoodcamera.com
(303-797-0700) Littleton, CO.

TABLE OF CONTENTS

CHAPTER ONE 8
My First Property

CHAPTER TWO 10
South Florida-Miami

CHAPTER THREE 24
I Build the Green House in Illinois

CHAPTER FOUR 31
My First House in Colorado

CHAPTER FIVE 34
New House in Aurora

CHAPTER SIX 38
Back in Littleton

CHAPTER SEVEN 42
Building Our House in the Foothills

CHAPTER EIGHT 48
My First Spec House

CHAPTER NINE 53
2nd Spec House

CHAPTER TEN 58
A Major Flip in Littleton

CHAPTER ELEVEN. 66
   A Flip in Englewood

CHAPTER TWELVE 70
   I Flip a Townhome

CHAPTER THIRTEEN. 74
   My First Land Parcel Flip

CHAPTER FOURTEEN 78
   The Big Flip

CHAPTER FIFTEEN 88
   Land, A Good Buy

CHAPTER SIXTEEN 94
   A Small Lot in Englewood

CHAPTER SEVENTEEN 100
   I Buy Another Large Property

CHAPTER EIGHTEEN. 112
   I Rent a Commercial Space

About the Author 113

CHAPTER ONE

My First Property
A Farm House in Illinois

I bought my first piece of Real Estate when I was in my early 20s from my Mom. She was moving to the city to be closer to work. It was located outside a small town. I paid $10,000.00 for it. It was a two story with a detached garage and small acreage.

I recall a time I was in the formal dining room and could feel fresh air. I investigated to see where it came from as it was winter.

After a short investigation, I discovered one corner of the wood frame around the window was completely rotted away, and the air was coming in from outside. I fixed it with some wood filler and called it a day.

This was in my youth. I didn't do any improvements to the property and sold it.

Sold, Closed, On to the Next.

CHAPTER TWO

2nd Property
South Florida-Miami
Bought November 1972

My next adventure was in South Florida.

It was winter in Illinois, so I decided to go back to Florida and look up my friend who I had gone down with the previous year.

The first year we went down together our plans were to help build Disney World. When we got there, we were told they had all the people they needed. We headed to Miami.

I was going to look for construction work again through the winter. We had rented a place together the first year.

Since the last winter when I was in Florida, he had bought a house and found a girlfriend.

I was raised on a 350-acre farm and need my elbow room, which I also call space.

I rented a room in a large apartment building. I knew after a few days it wasn't going to work for me. The size, noise, all the people coming and going during the night at all times.

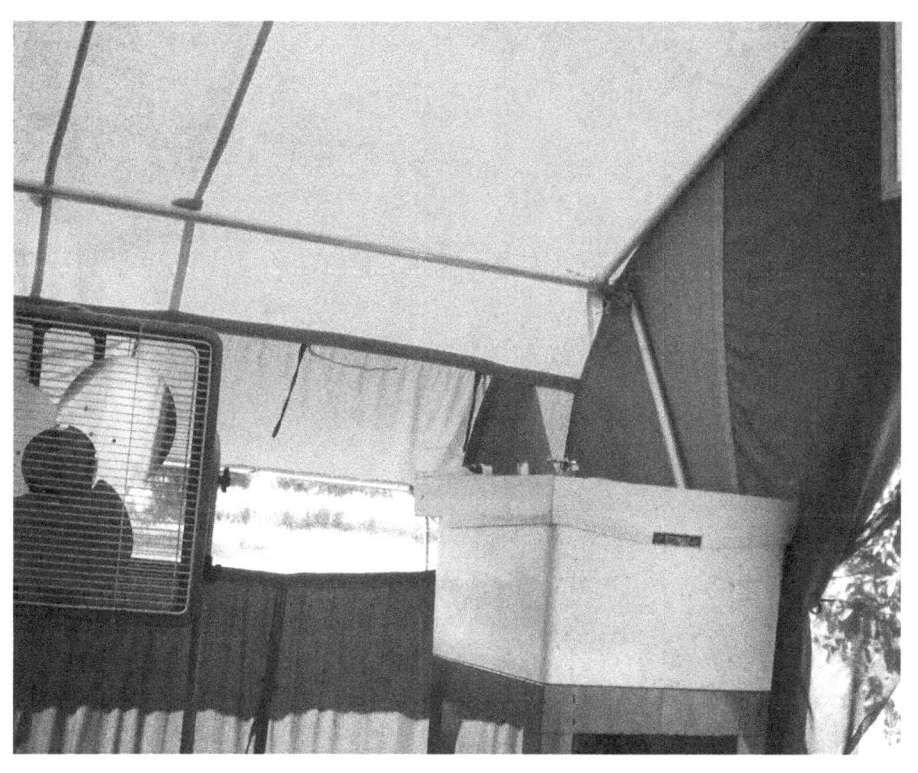

I mentioned this to my friend. He had a small house on acreage. He suggested putting up a tent in his back yard.

That is what we did. He grew a garden and planted corn toward the back. Behind the corn we put up my tent. We dug two trenches from his house to my tent and put in electrical and water lines. The tent was canvas and 9 × 12.

We put it on cement blocks with a plywood platform. I bought linoleum to cover the plywood, a utility sink, a fan, a small refrigerator, and a fold-up bed. I bought a hot plate for meals. I had my home. I lived there for a few months until the property next door came up for sale.

A next door neighbor decided to sell his property. This small area had older homes with acreage. It was a newer house than the others, made of cinder blocks with plaster over the exterior. The supporting columns were poured concrete to support a second story if the owner would want to add a second story in the future.

It was a fixer upper. Time to move from my tent.

I put a down payment down and the owner carried the balance with monthly payments until I had paid him in full the balance of the loan he was carrying, or I sold it before, and he would get the balance owed him at closing.

I had it a few years and fixed it some. First thing was to clean up the landscaping. Other than almost nothing but weeds, it also had an old car sitting in the front yard that I needed to get rid of. After that was cleaned up it was time to paint. I must have looked on weekends for weeks looking for the right exterior color. I finally found the color I thought was perfect, yellow. After it was prepped and painted, the color looked like baby s**t yellow. After all the time I had taken looking for a color, I left it. I didn't do much else on the outside and nothing on the inside. There was a canal in the back with a small deck and came with an alligator. In the back yard was a mango tree and a lemon tree. Trees lined the other side of the canal. As this was an older area, it had mature trees on the properties. It was a very secluded area.

Paradise in the big city.

I decided to go back to Illinois. I rented the house to the brother and some of his friends of a guy I worked with for a couple years. That didn't work out well.

I decided to sell it. A Real Estate agent came by and said if I could get more of the neighbors interested in selling there would be a better chance to sell and get more money per lot. That R.E. agent couldn't find a buyer. After a while another agent found a buyer, and the group of us that agreed to sell their properties as a group sold it to Florida Power and Light for a sub-station. I was back in Illinois when it closed. I had a Power of Attorney represent me at the closing. When I received the check after expenses, I made money. I thought this was o.k.

Florida Power and Light apparently changed their mind, as it is a large church campus now.

Sold January 1975

Sold, Closed, Made money, On to the Next.

CHAPTER THREE

I Build the Green House
in Illinois
Bought June 1975

After I was back in Illinois and got settled, I went to see a friend I hadn't seen for a while since I had been in Florida. In the past when I needed a job, this friend had hired me to help with his gas station. I pumped customers gas, checked their engine oil, cleaned their windshield, and made sure the tires looked like they had proper air pressure in them.

During our visit he told me he had bought a house just outside of town. I wanted to see it and we set a time for me to meet him and take a look. When I got to his house, I was really impressed. It was a large brick ranch with a swimming pool and sat on an acre. While we were walking around his property, I noticed an empty lot next to his. I asked him about it, and he didn't know who owned it as there was no Realtor sign. I used his address and went to the county building and looked up who owned it in county records. I contacted the owner and we came to terms on the purchase price.

There were only six lots in this whole subdivision just outside of town.

After I bought my lot there was just one left.

I now owned an acre that had a well. I paid $5,700.00 for it.

Another of my friends had built a house that I liked in a different town.

It was 1,500 square feet with three bedrooms, a full bath plus another 3/4 bath, and a two-car garage. I decided to build a house like his. His dad was a 3rd-generation builder contractor and I hired him to build it.

Building the Green House

There is a lot to building a house from scratch which I didn't know, but was about to find out. As I said before, I contracted with my friend's dad and his crew. I thought how hard could it be since it is a duplicate of the house they built for his son.

Everything was the same except of course the location and the interior finish. I was about to find out. They used T-squares to cut the angles/pitches on the rafters. This is an art form used on dimensional lumber. Nowadays they are manufactured on a different site and trucked to the property most of the time. As I recall the only bad thing that happened was the subcontractor that was putting in the leach field for the septic tank, cut through the power line with their backhoe. The power company had already laid it in the ground. They didn't call for utility locations in the ground like they should have.

The house was framed and the contractor came to me one day and asked me about the front door.

I asked what he meant and this is what he asked:

Which way do you want the door to swing? I thought, this will be easy.

Then he asked;

Do you want a wood, metal, or fiberglass front door?

Do you want it smooth skinned or panels? If panels how many?

Do you want glass at the top, and if you do, what style do you want?

Do you want a doorknob or handle?

What type of finish; black, brown, nickel, or—?

I was about to lose my mind and then he asked, what color?

This was just for the front door.

How hard could it be to build a house—plenty.

My mom and sister were a big help with staining, wall papering, and landscape planting.

It finally got built. I was really proud. I lived in it for a year or two and also rented it, as I would go back to Florida to work in the winter.

My "forever home," or so I thought.

I was a construction worker operating heavy equipment.

There wasn't much work around so I took a trip to Colorado to visit a friend.

I liked Colorado so much that I came back to Illinois to settle things, rent the "green house," pack, and I moved to Colorado.

I have many good memories with the "green house," named that because the siding was green.

While in Colorado I made the decision to stay there permanently and decided to sell the "green house."

I didn't like the commission per centage Realtors were getting so I hired an auction company to sell it for me. It was sold while I was in Colorado.

To this day, I don't know if I made the right decision in hiring an auction company or if I should have gone with a Realtor.

Sold April 1979

Sold, Closed, Made money, On to the Next.

CHAPTER FOUR

My First House in Colorado
Bought September 1979

I like to have my money build value. That is why I lived in a tent for a while in Florida.

I moved to Colorado in 1978. I stayed with my friend off and on and also rented a room from a person I had met while working a construction job.

Now that I was getting more settled, it was time to look for a house to buy. I would drive around on weekends to different areas of Denver. I liked the South area and bought my first property in Littleton with the money I made from the sale of the house in Illinois and the property in Florida.

It needed updating which I never did other than painting. I rented the upstairs for extra money and some friends and I called the basement home.

After a few years I decided to sell it and bought a new house from a builder in Aurora.

Sold April 1982

Sold, Closed, Made money, On to the Next.

CHAPTER FIVE

New House in Aurora
Bought September 1982

It was a four-level house which I had never heard of. From what I heard, when builders were starting a new subdivision, they would do a few random soil samples on the whole area. This is how the foundation design is determined—what it takes so the house won't settle or move.

During the walk-through I had three and a half pages of things that needed to be addressed. Most of the things got done. I would have waited until all was done, but had closed on the Littleton house and needed to move in. I remember arguing with the builder's representative that the real cedar shake shingles needed oil on them to preserve them longer so they wouldn't dry out. It never got done by them.

I would always do a walk through before the closing. Sometimes you can't get everything done that needs to be done before closing because of the lock on your loan, sold your other house and need to move in quick, your furniture is arriving, the market is hot, and if you don't close someone else will buy it just to name a few.

Builders want to get it sold and closed so they can get it off their books. Make a list of what needs to be addressed and try to get it all done before you move in. Bring pen and paper when doing your inspection and a flashlight.

If you are working with a contractor who is building your house, you should be able to work with them more closely with items that need to be addressed than a large builder.

Once you approve the blueprints, if you are doing the building, try to keep it the way it is. If you do change orders, that's where it can get expensive, especially if the work has already been done. Larger changes will probably have to be approved by the building department which can take time, money, and slow down construction time. That being said, if it is something you can't live with, make the changes. After it is built is not the time to change something, especially if it is a wall or something structural.

We have a soil type called bentonite in parts of Colorado. It's a type of clay that expands when wet and shrinks when dry. If this happens it can damage your bottom floor. I've personally seen what it does to floors.

My lower floor heaved. It was from the soil expanding. A company came in, jack hammered the concrete out, dug down about two feet and excavated all the dirt within the foundation, put gravel down, installed wood floor joists with plywood on top, and installed a dehumidifier. This way if the soil expanded again, it had room to expand under the floor as they had dug it down two feet and created a void.

I had moved to Colorado to be close to the mountains. This house had been closer to work, but the pull from the mountains was too strong.

I put the house up for sale. At this time FHA and VA loans could be assumed. I had an FHA loan.

I sold it to an Army vet. He paid me a small down payment on my equity I had in it and assumed my FHA loan. He was responsible for payments to the bank and me for the balance of the equity I was carrying. He stopped making payments to the bank and me. He had a disability income from the military so I had thought he would be able to make the payments. I took him to small claims court for what he owed me. I won and then the judge said good luck getting it. I thought I could garnish his military disability. I got an attorney to try and get it. Found out at the time it happened you can't garnish disabilities or Social Security. That might have changed by now, but that is what I was told then.

FHA took over the house loan.

Sold October 1986

Lost Money! On to the Next.

CHAPTER SIX

Back in Littleton
Bought June 1987

It feels good to be back by the Foothills.

My girlfriend had been living with me and driving a long way to work. I wanted to get closer to the mountains, the reason I moved to Colorado. She found a rental in Littleton. When we pulled in front, I looked at her and shook my head. It was painted a dark red purple. From what we were living in and to move into this small fixer-upper? We did. We rented it and moved in. It was a small ranch house that needed work.

After a while we decided we wanted to buy a place. We talked to our landlords to see if they wanted to sell and they said yes. We agreed on a purchase price and now owned a home back in Littleton. It was small, but cozy and comfortable.

Over the years I put on a new roof (the inspector told me it was one of the best jobs he had ever inspected), painted it twice, new water heater, new furnace, and new cedar fencing on the front and sides. We planted a maple tree in front along with some bushes and did some planting in back.

We discussed if we stayed, we would need to replace the single pane windows with double pane windows, new cabinets, add a master bedroom with a master bath, and of course a two-car garage for me as it only had a single-car garage. We knew it would take a long time to do all this and wondered if we would get our money back should we decide to sell in the future. One morning (I had married my girlfriend) I rolled over in bed and told her I wanted to build a house. This way we could get what we wanted. I started looking for a lot to build on. I looked at many and found one that would work. It was a "For Sale By Owner." I had a contract on it, but it fell through. We are so glad it did. Another better property came up for sale and we bought it. Sometimes it just works out.

We put the Littleton house on the market and had it sold within three days at our full asking price. You wonder, was the price too low or was it just the house they wanted and didn't want someone else to get it? We should have asked more maybe, but also it could have taken a lot longer to sell. To my knowledge, to this day they still own it twenty-seven years later. We stayed there for 11 years. Again, many fond memories.

Sold September 1995

Sold, Closed, Made money, On to the Next.

CHAPTER SEVEN

Building Our House in the Foothills
Bought January 1995

Before we sold the Littleton house, we had bought the Foothills property. The Florida property, the green house, Aurora house, and Littleton house all had large lots. This is what we were looking for and found.

We hired an architect to design blueprints which needed to be stamped with approval by the county. We submitted the blueprints and they came back with a few items that needed to be changed. Once this was finished, we had our blueprints approved.

We had started building before we sold the Littleton house. Since our Foothills home wasn't finished, we had to rent. We knew it would be a short term as our house was close to being done. We found a place to rent and glad we didn't have to stay there long.

The owner lost our rent check and didn't pay the water bill. We called the owner to tell him we didn't have any water and he said he forgot to pay the bill, go next door.

The lot sloped a little to the south and was 12,770 square feet. It had lots of smaller trees, which I liked coming from a farm that had many.

They call it a "take off" meaning what you will need to frame the house. We sat down with the estimator, gave him a copy of our blueprints, and sat back. After briefly looking them over, he looked up and asked, do you really want to do this? My wife and I looked at each other and then asked, what do you mean? He said he had worked with a young couple to build their dream home, and they ended up getting a divorce. We told him to go ahead.

If you hire a general contractor, you won't realize how many different subcontractors it takes to build a house. You'll find out if you become the general contractor.

Be sure to carry insurance on the house, even when the house isn't done. Things that could happen are tornadoes, wind, fire, vandalism, theft, etc.

Take photos of the different stages and there are a lot. While building your home there will be a lot of memories. One of many that sticks out in my mind after working on the house until dark, I got a beer and sat on the front porch. I looked out to the west and saw a lightning show I had never experienced before. I called a company the next day and had lightning rods installed on the roof.

While we were building our house, we both had full-time jobs, mine being 30 minutes from the job site. I can see where it can be tough on you.

Just before we started building, I joined a class on building construction. I would rush to the class after work to get there on time.

It wasn't close to the building site. When not in class I would rush to the site to see what the contractors had got done that day. I would do what I could before it got dark to save money. We moved in December of 1995. We are still there, December 2023.

This is a photo of a cast iron tub we had reporcelained. Three of us tried to get it up the inside stairs and couldn't. It was just too heavy. I hired a crane truck to lift it up and swing it over the railing so we could get it to the guest bathroom.

CHAPTER EIGHT

My First Spec House
Bought October 1996

The challenge was there. I decided to build a spec house although I was still working full time. For those who don't know, a spec house is a speculation house. You speculate that when you sell it, after all costs, you will make money for your time and risk.

I still had my Real Estate license and since I wasn't getting any listings, I decided to build my listing. When sold, I would then get the listing commission.

I found another lot in our neighborhood. I had plans drawn up somewhat like our house so it wouldn't cost so much to pay an architect to start from scratch.

With our personal house, I rehired some of the subcontractors that had worked on it-not all. One contractor stands out the most.

He was a drywaller and had done a great job on our house. Not only was the work quality, he and his crew showed up on time. He came by and gave me an estimate and I rehired him. After work that day I stopped by to see how things went. I was in shock. Where they sprayed the walls was ok, but there was a mess on the floor, and walls in

the garage where they had mixed the mud. When they sprayed the walls going downstairs, they didn't cover the basement floor or the basement wall. There was drywall mud on the floor and the basement wall where the stairs met. I knew I wasn't going to clean it up.

When you get a construction loan there are many items on the draw list. You call up your loan officer, tell them what has been done and they send someone out to take pictures and verify it has been done. You then give the loan officer the invoices from the subs and they will give you the checks to disburse. I knew what to do. I had heard too many stories about contractors saying they would get someone out to fix it, or they just didn't currently have the time. O.K. I thought. I called my banker and told him on the drywall invoice I want you to make two checks. One for eighty percent of the invoice and the other for twenty per cent.

I sent the eighty percent out. I received a call from the contractor saying what's going on? I explained to him the mess that was left, and I wasn't going to pay the other twenty percent until it was cleaned up. I don't recall if it was that afternoon or the next day his crew was out there cleaning it up. I had control and didn't have to listen to excuses. He had gotten so busy he had hired another company to do his work. If you contract with a company, be sure you know if they are doing the work or if they will sub it out to another company. I didn't hire him for my next house.

There are different textures with drywall; orange peel, knockdown, etc. Orange peel is pretty constant, but you can do a medium or heavy knockdown texture. If doing the knockdown, I would suggest being there the day they spray the texture as it will be on all the walls you choose. For you and the sprayer person to be on the same page, I would suggest to start the texture spraying in a closet so you both can agree on the spray texture if it needs to be adjusted.

This way if the texture starts too heavy, you can scrape it off the wall while wet and reset the texture spray to lighter.

Same thing happened with the painting company. I believe he said he hired his uncle.

The day the drywall was delivered there was frost in the ground. The front sloped to the street. The delivery truck pulled in on the front yard. While they were unloading, the sun came out, the frost started to go and the dirt got slippery. They took out the water meter getting out as they slid into it.

Where I live you need inspections on the work that is done. I called and set up a time for the inspector to come do a walk through. He came out and saw a few things that needed to be fixed so it would meet the code book regulations they use. I got the issues fixed and called for my last inspection to get my C.O.—Certificate of Occupancy. A different inspector came out. He approved all the fixes. He found a few other things that needed work. The basement was open. The south end was a garden level which if you stood on the basement floor, the ground outside the window was four inches below the window sill. This way if there was a fire a person could just climb out the window. On the other end the ground was higher so I had put in a large window well. As this was an unfinished basement,

I felt the level on the south end was o.k. If a fire happened, they could climb to safety to the ground four inches below the window sill. Nope, not this inspector. He said I needed a ladder in the four-foot window well so people could get out if needed. I said it is an open unfinished basement. He looked at me and said, Do you want your C.O.? After he left, I was driving up Santa Fe to buy a metal ladder to put in the window well. After this I received my C.O. after another inspection to ensure I had done everything.

Moral of this episode; different people have different opinions and view things differently.

I talked to one general contractor and told him my story. He said if you build a working relationship with an inspector always ask for the same one. You need to remember if she or he is sick or on vacation it might be weeks before they can come back. At the end of construction and you are looking for your C.O., interest on your loan will be adding up on the loan amount you have running. Sometimes it's better to just keep moving forward.

I first tried to sell it For Sale By Owner so I wouldn't have to pay a selling commission to the Real Estate agent that brings a buyer. That didn't work out, so I listed it.

Sold November 1997

Sold, Closed, Made money, On to the Next.

CHAPTER NINE

2nd Spec House
Bought May 1998

I still had the bug to build another spec house. I found and bought another lot. I wanted to come down in price, and the time it took to build the two story, so this time I built a ranch house.

One of the issues I remember with this build was the roofing company I hired. They had different crews do different work. The felt crew did their work, the shingle crew did their work, and the gutter crew almost did their work. It was all done, but in the back one corner had not been completed. We had a big rain and eroded a large area of yard as it was all coming down out of the corner with no erosion control.

I was tired of picking colors so I went with the color I had painted our house and my first spec.

I hired a neighbor to help me with meeting the subs. I would tell this person who was coming, when, and what I wanted done so I wouldn't have to take time off work. This didn't work out. They didn't have any experience with construction, so I still had to do a lot of calls and take time off.

I was still the general contractor with a full-time job 30 minutes away from the site.

Sold March 1999

Sold, Closed, Made money, On to the Next.

CHAPTER TEN

A Major Flip in Littleton
Bought May 2008

I took a break for a few years not buying any Real Estate. Then 2008 came around and I got the bug again. I started looking for a house that was already built, but needed help. I knew I could kill it with my building experience.

I looked for a while and found a house that was a fix up in Littleton. I bought it and started work.

When you build a new home, do a flip, or remodel, you sometimes get a loan. You can look at this in different ways; you can pay people to do the work/ it will cost more in labor, but will get done sooner (hopefully), reducing the interest on the loan, or you and friends can do the work-cheaper labor, but will take longer probably increasing the time of the loan and increasing the cost of the loan as the interest on the loan is running longer.

I like to make my properties pop. I like to stand out in the competition.

I had new windows put in, painted inside and out, fencing, updated plumbing and electrical, some flooring replaced, new kitchen with cabinets and appliances along with granite counter tops, all new bathrooms with lighting,

flooring, tile, toilet, tub, sink, fixtures-new sod, sprinkler system, and finished the basement to code.

On the final electrical inspection in the kitchen, the inspector pointed something out and said if you would have called next week that wouldn't have passed. They were upgrading their code book the next week.

I added a legal bedroom in the basement by cutting out an egress opening for an escape window in the bedroom to make it legal. It had a three-car garage with just a two-garage door opening. The other area was for storage. I had another garage door installed. I had most of the work done professionally. I had spent most of the summer working on it.

It looked GREAT. I was going to kill it.

Two weeks after it was on the Real Estate market, 2008 reared its ugly head when most everything crashed.

Most of the larger financial corps, insurance companies, and many others failed.

After a month of it being listed and watching the value go down, I decided to rent it until the market turned around.

I had great tenants the first couple years. Then it changed. All good things come to an end.

I got the bad tenants out and got new ones.

They paid, but there were issues. I gave them notice to move out as I was going to sell. The market had changed some.

To evict them and actually have them move out are two different things.

There was a girl who had been living in the basement. I knew the guy had moved out. Luckily, I went over there with my wife. We went over to see what it looked like and what we would have to do to fix it up. I had the key and we went in. I announced ourselves and didn't hear a reply. After walking the top floor, we went down in the basement.

The girl came out and I asked what she was still doing there. She said she was still moving out. My wife and I left. When we got home, I received a call from the police department. She called the police on us.

I was so glad I had my wife with me as a witness. She could have accused me of a lot of things. It would have been up to me to prove she was lying. Wonder if she had a fight with her boyfriend the night before and had bruises?

Note—when evicting someone or checking on a rental, take a witness with you.

Finally, she was out. Time to repaint and redo floors. The landscaping was a disaster.

One of the tenants said they had a small dog. If you are renting a property to a tenant, I would suggest you see the dog, put a weight and how many are allowed, and if the amount and/or size exceeds the contract agreement, this is cause for you to get them out due to breaking the contract they agreed to.

I had one tenant say they had a small dog and I took their word for it. Later when I saw their dog, he had gained about hundred pounds in two months.

I couldn't stand to lose the money we had in the house.
We rented it for five years until the market turned around.

Sold June 2013

Sold, Closed, Came Out About Even.

CHAPTER ELEVEN

A Flip in Englewood
Bought June 2014

After a year the Real Estate bug bit me again. I told my wife I wanted to invest again and she supported me on the idea.

My wife mentioned it to a friend and she knew her neighbor was getting ready to sell their property.

I drove by the property, and it looked so bad I didn't even go in. I thought I would clear the lot and tear the house down.

The owners hired a Realtor to protect them in the contract, and I hired and paid a Realtor to protect my legal interests. The owners and I agreed to terms, signed a contract and I owned a fix up with a large lot. There was a lot to do just to clean the lot and empty the house.

There was so much inside the house, instead of tearing it down, I decided to clean it out and maybe find some treasures of value. I didn't.

It took three-four roll offs to carry off everything that was in the house and clean the lot. After the inside was empty, I took a look around. It was a small house and had been added on to not very well.

I didn't want to put money into it to fix it up at this point, as I didn't feel I could get a good return on my investment.

I listed it with my Realtor and fully expected a builder would come in, tear the house down, and build a large new house. Nope, it was bought by another flipper. They fixed it up and sold it.

I did hear one of the roofers fell through the roof. You see why I thought it would be torn down.

You just don't know other people's vision.

If it is not falling down and safe, go inside, but with another person or two and maybe a hard hat. Have a flashlight, pen and paper and take notes. If you expect mold, have a licensed company go in and check it.

Sold October 2014

Sold, Closed, Made money, The Spark is Back, On to the Next.

Not staged.

CHAPTER TWELVE

I Flip a Townhome
Bought October 2015

When you are looking to flip, you need to find deals so you can make money after all the costs are deducted. If you are looking for a project, you need to be looking all the time.

This townhome had fallen out of the contract it was under and came back on the market. It came back the morning I saw it on my computer. I called my Realtor and she made an appointment for a showing that day. Later that day I made an offer and that night I owned a townhome.

It needed updating, but wasn't too bad.

We put in an all-new kitchen and baths, paint, flooring, replaced one window, and patched the holes in the walls.

When fixing a flip or your personal home, I would suggest you keep all the hardware.

I threw some items away as I was going to order replacements, but then found out I couldn't get the replacements. The company hadn't picked up the roll-off and I was able to find what I needed.

I hired a video person to film different stages of remodeling and I put it on YouTube.

Sold March 2016

Sold, Closed, Made money, On to the Next.

CHAPTER THIRTEEN

My First Land Parcel Flip
Bought September 2017

I was looking for another residential property to flip. A new listing came up on a Saturday morning. I called my Realtor to set up a showing. I met her there and we walked the house. Then we went in the basement. One of the walls had a large crack in it that I thought was maybe a structural issue.

When we got upstairs, I told my Realtor I wasn't interested because of what I saw in the basement. While I was talking to her, I was facing the sliding glass door looking out back. There was a large empty lot. I asked my Realtor if she would call the listing agent and ask her if she knew who the owner was.

My Realtor called the listing agent and was told the property belonged to the owner of the house and hadn't got it listed yet. I asked my Realtor to ask what they were going to list it for. The listing agent said she would have to get back after talking to the owner. My Realtor called me later that afternoon and told me what the price was.

I had it under contract that night.

There was a nice shed and a small gazebo with some benches and a small garden area framed with railroad ties. I tore down the gazebo and left the shed and the railroad ties.

I sold it to a custom home builder who built a huge house on it.

Sold November 2017

Sold, Closed, Made money, On to the Next.

CHAPTER FOURTEEN

The Big Flip
Bought February 2018

If you are working with a good Realtor they will keep their eyes and ears open. I was looking for another property to flip when my Realtor called to say an agent in her company was listing a house I might want to look at.

Oh boy!!! I don't know how people can live in what I saw. I was hungry for something to do. I made an offer and they accepted.

Note: just because the seller (s) drop the price a large amount doesn't mean it's a good deal. I didn't realize until later I paid too much. In saying that, I don't take short cuts. I fix the properties I buy like my wife and I are going to live in them. I could have saved a lot of money if I hadn't retextured all the existing drywall, but felt it needed it with all the patches that showed.

This was a bigger house, lots bigger that my first flip and the townhome. It needed a lot of work. I hired some laborers to help clear the inside and clean the yard. It took three to four roll-offs. We packed the trash in the roll-offs. If we hadn't and just thrown the trash in it would have taken at least another roll-off. Then I saw what I had bought. A lot more work than what I had envisioned. Well, it was mine so let's get started.

Once all the loose items were gone, we started on the bathrooms and the kitchen. They had their washer and dryer in the kitchen. I redesigned the kitchen in that area for a pantry and moved the hook ups for the washer and dryer to the basement.

The doorway to the dining room was narrow and that wall was non-supporting. Be sure when opening a door way, window, or a wall it is not load bearing. When in doubt call a structural engineer or talk to your contractor. I opened it a little to allow more room when walking into the dining room from the kitchen. While in the kitchen, we took the ceiling down as the shower above leaked.

I got some referrals from friends on some contractors. One wasn't showing up. I called and complained. He told me he had to take care of his large customers first. No, when you agree to do a job, you do it and don't leave your customer like that. I fired him.

I did a new kitchen and bathrooms, new drywall texture, flooring, new windows except the bay window, upgraded plumbing, upgraded electrical, new A/C unit, new fence, new driveway and walkway, new garage door, new interior doors and trim for the doors and baseboard trim. Redesigned shelving by the fireplace with a new mantel. I had the air vents cleaned, the furnace serviced, and the house professionally cleaned. I also had new gutters and downspouts installed.

I used all my home equity, some savings, and started using my credit cards to get it done.

There was some work to be done in the back sun room. I felt instead of doing this I would discount the asking price. This didn't work. I took it off the market, found some more money, fixed what was needed and put it back on the market. It hadn't been on the market long and I received an offer with a letter from the family who had made the offer with a picture of the family and saying how much they loved the house. We countered on price a little and came to terms. The walk through with their inspector found some things and said we will have them fixed, but you need to reduce the price so we will have the money to pay for it.

I wasn't in a position to go back and forth, and the buying season was about over for the summer.

I bought it in February and closed in August. I was there every day but three working.

I knew about scheduling, timing and how interest adds up on loans. Looking back, I think I just tried to do too much on my own and owned it too long.

Lesson learned. Old dogs can learn from their mistakes!

Sold August 2018

Sold, Closed, Didn't Make Money, On to the Next?

Not staged.

Not staged.

Not staged.

CHAPTER FIFTEEN

Land, A Good Buy
Bought December 2018

As I said before, if you are going to be an investor, you have to always be looking. Let people know you are actively looking to buy.

I couldn't help myself. I started looking for another property.

I saw the listing the first day it was on the market. It was close to where I live, so I drove over immediately. I liked it. I called my Realtor and we put in an offer. My offer was low, I was testing to see what they would come back at. The seller countered close to the original asking price. I accepted, as I knew this lot was a good buy even at the price I agreed to. We had an agreement within 48 hours.

There was nothing to do to it. No trash removal, no taking down any buildings. It was a large flat lot. Easy to build on and located on a quiet street that ended in a cul-de-sac with a view of the Foothills, if the buyer (s) would build a two story which they did.

One day I thought I had better go take a look to be sure trash wasn't being dumped on the site. This was a lot with houses around it. No trash, but I noticed I needed to find a company to mow the weeds as they had gotten

high. I found a company that would do the mowing, and they said they would drive by and give me an estimate. I called them a few days later to get their price.

To my surprise they said it had already been mowed. I went over and went up to a neighbor's house to ask who mowed the lot. I said I wasn't upset, just wanted to give the person some money for doing it. He said the guy across the street. I went over and introduced myself, thanked him for mowing it, and offered him some money. He told me I didn't have to, and I told him, yes I did.

I knew I had a good lot, so I kept it for over a year. This is treated in this writing as long term capital gains which you are taxed at a lower rate.

I listed it on Zillow and didn't say anything about offering a commission to a Realtor. I had a few calls, but no serious offers. Then one day I received a call from a Realtor. He said his clients had noticed my ad. He asked if I would take a lower price. I said no, I had been offered a lower price before and didn't take it. He asked if I would pay a commission to him and I said yes, call my Realtor.

Real Estate deals can be complex so I always hire a Realtor to protect my interest via a contract.

I was happy and the buyers were happy. They built a beautiful home.

Even with all the properties I have owned, I made a mistake.

The Realtor's buyer(s) found the property, he didn't. I agreed to pay the normal commission at the time. I should have negotiated his commission lower. I didn't.

Old dogs can learn from their mistakes!

Sold March 2020

Sold, Closed, Made money, On to the Next.

CHAPTER SIXTEEN

A Small Lot in Englewood
Bought November 2020

It took a while to find another project. I am always looking. One morning I found another property that had fallen out of contract that morning. I drove over to take a look. I thought it had potential. I made an offer, they countered, I countered and they accepted. Now I had time to do my due diligence.

Although the listing said public sewer and water, I confirmed that with the city department. While I was talking to them, I was told the permit fees were going up in a couple months. I had thought I would tear the old house down and build a rental unit. I told my Realtor to cancel the contract due to the coming increase in permits. The sellers accepted that fact as they had their Realtor call to confirm it, and they accepted my lower adjusted offer.

First, I cut some trees down to open up the lot to make it look bigger. There was a large dead tree in back. To make it look more marketable it needed to go. It was at the back of my lot and at the edge of the owners who sold me the lot. I went to them and said I'll pay for half to take it down if you pay for the other half. They discussed it and agreed.

By this time, I had decided to sell it and not tear the old house in the back down.

A Realtor investor bought it and built a spec house.

Sold March 2021

Sold, Closed, Made money, On to the Next.

CHAPTER SEVENTEEN

I Buy Another Large Property
Bought October 31, 2023.

As I stated earlier, you always need to be looking.

I saw it the first day it was listed.

I drove by, liked it, and called my Realtor.

I had it under contract within two days.

This book was just getting ready to go to the publisher when I found this property.

It's clear of any buildings and county records say it is 13,097 square feet in size.

I had to add chapter seventeen.

Glad I did!

Thank you for buying and reading my book. I hope you enjoyed it, learned some things, and was entertained from my experiences.

Things to think about and remember: So, you want to build, add on to your place, remodel, or flip a property.

When buying land or a lot to build on, get a copy of the covenants, and if it has an HOA, a copy of those as well to see if they will work for you. Sometimes you have to use their builders. Check this out along with zoning and building codes. Ask if permit costs are going up anytime in the near future or tap fees if you will be hooking up to public services.

Years back I heard Boulder wouldn't let you put real shake shingles on your roof because of fires. If you wanted real shakes you'd have to look elsewhere.

In all the years I've been involved with Real Estate, I've only given a few contractors money up front to start the project. Lots of the established contractors have credit with their material suppliers. With the credit earned by good repayments of supplies they bought before, the supply house will usually give them at least thirty days to pay for the supplies they've charged.

This might have changed, but it was like this. For smaller jobs, if the contractor needs to buy materials, go with them to the store and YOU buy the materials and have them delivered if you don't have a vehicle to transport the materials, or follow your contractor with the supplies back to your place with the material and unload the material you bought.

This way you have the supplies you paid for and if the contractor doesn't show up you can look for a different one.

Be sure to protect your supplies from theft and weather.

Both parties need to agree on how payment is going to be made and when.

If you are looking to build on a lot/land, some things to check out. Before purchasing the land, look into how deep the wells are being drilled to get water if you don't have public water. When buying you want to visualize how you want your home to face. If buying in a cul-de-sac, ask about the setbacks from the front and side property lines. The further you have to go back to meet these setbacks, the further you may get from public water and sewer if this is offered. If not a well and septic system, to get to the public main lines will cost you more for materials and labor as now your home is further back and you have to run your lines further.

I would get an idea of the style of home, if you are building a new one, then start looking for land that it will work on.

We had our garage door built 18' wide so when we have both cars in the garage, we have room to open the doors. That is an extra 2 feet so it will cost more, but we like the space.

Knowing how to size your new build if designing it yourself; I would go to a park or place of your choosing. If in a park, go to an area where no one is using it and take rolls of pink ribbon you can buy at a big box store and a roll up fifty-foot tape. Have weights to hold corners as you stretch the ribbon out. Measure the rooms to what size you want. You are in the open. I would increase the size of the rooms by at least six inches each direction (and maybe more) after the initial layout. When you get the walls up the space will shrink.

There are other ways to do this, it's just difficult looking at a blueprint and deciding the rooms are the correct size. If adding on a space or new build, plan on a storage area for holiday decorations, sports equipment, etc. Decide what size appliances you will have as you measure the space out. Layout the size of your furniture in the rooms.

Be sure when leaving to take your ribbon and weights.

When doing the cabinets, do you want the hinges to show, knobs or handles?

I would get at least 3 written bids from contractors.

Subject to the size of your house, which in turn depends on how long it will take to build, you may want to buy some of the interior trim pieces you found and liked (electrical and plumbing) when you start. By the time you get to installing the finishes the company may be out of business or the manufacture may not be in business any longer and you may not be able to buy what you saw and wanted months earlier.

Remember doing this is using up your cash early or increasing your loan on the build which will cost you extra interest early on for your loan.

If you don't do this, I would have three choices of each so when it comes time and you can't find your first choice, you already have backups, and you won't have to hurry to find a replacement.

Again, if you do any changes in part of the construction, do it before it gets done. If you do changes after it's done, it will be expensive to change it.

If you can't live with the way it will be, change it.

If you build a ranch style, how will your views be if someone on the empty lot next to yours builds a two story?

Landscape; if you have a slope close to the back of your home, (and the property belongs to you) try and move the foot of the slope back, build a sturdy wall with drainage, maybe going into a French drain.

See your builder, engineer, or architect.

It will probably be a good idea to install a sump pump if you have a basement or crawl space.

Some people put edging around their house three to four feet out from the foundation. Due to rain you want to keep the water away from your foundation, so you don't have problems in your basement or crawl space. Most downspout extensions are three to four feet in length. It gets old removing them when mowing. You can cut them at the top by the elbow to swing them up out of the way. You will need to put a screw in each side so it acts like a hinge. If you hear of any big storms, you may want to slide a round plastic pipe over the end of the extension pipe to get water further away from the foundation. Lift the end of the extension and slide the round tube about a foot back. Make sure you still have the extension and tube slope away from the foundation.

Have your home sit higher than the ground around it so water drains away from your foundation naturally if building new.

If you have trees by the house, clean your gutters so the rain off the roof can get down the downspout and run through the extension and away from the foundation.

Painting; so your paint brush doesn't hit bottom in what you are using to hold your paint, drill a small hole below the metal on the brush and screw in a cup holder hook. You may have to open the hook end so as to hook it on the edge of your paint container. This way the paint bristles won't bend having it rest on the bottom. You will have to adjust this to your liking and what side to mount it on.

I use to get paint all the way up the brush bristles by the metal. Now I use blue paint tape and cover the top 3/8 inch or so of the bristles to keep the paint out. This depends on the size of brush you are using. Don't apply the tape too far down from the bottom of the metal or the bristles will not be flexible.

Roll-offs: large metal containers for trash that are delivered by trucks. Containers are rolled off a truck track.

Drywall can have square or round (bullnose) corners. I was told if you have a lot of round corners, it will cost more for labor and drywall mud. I like round corners in doorways. I like the feeling, like it is inviting you into the next room.

For windows, if you are going to have curtains or drapes coming down and covering the corner areas, I would go with square corners as they will be covered.

If the sides will always be covered with curtains or drapes, I wouldn't put wood trim around the window, just the window sill. This may be different if you have a bay window.

This is up to your personal choice, but will cost more for the extra labor and material.

Windows are made of wood, vinyl, or a combination of each. If you decide on wood outside, after years they will probably have to be scraped and repainted. That isn't bad unless you have a two story. Lots of labor time to walk up and down the ladder and moving it.

Vinyl can fade over time, however it is much better quality than it once was.

There are sliders, single hung, double hung, and crank out style windows.

Sliders are the cheapest, then single hung, and then double hung. Single hung is a better option than double hung. Double hung, the bottom and top moves. Single hung is a better choice because it has a better R value because the top doesn't open. You can buy both of these windows with grids in them to prevent people from looking into your house. If you have a view, you don't want sliders because the frames will be in the middle of the view. It's up to you, which style and price point you choose. The top will probably be covered with a valance, curtain, or shade so you wouldn't get any breeze or air flow having a double hung.

Real Estate values going up is called appreciation. Going down is negative equity or called "under water."

Making an offer doesn't mean it will be accepted.

I was a licensed Realtor from 1980 to 2000. Real Estate doesn't always go up in value.

An old saying is; location, location, location.

I like to say terms can be added to the value.

Remember, things change; building and zoning codes, tax laws, interest rates, economy, etc.

One of my broker's told me (when I had my Real Estate license) there will always be buyers and sellers, no matter the interest rate, the economy, people moving, job relocation, downsizing, etc.

P.I.T.I. = Principle, Interest, Taxes, and Insurance

P.I.T.I.-even with a fixed interest rate it can go up due to higher taxes and/or insurance.

H.O.A.s can increase in cost also.

Generally, you need to have 20% of value in your home before you can drop mortgage insurance. Talk to your mortgage lender.

If you want to become a landlord, you should first look into what it takes legally to evict a non-payer. I've heard, subject to where you live, it may take thirty days or more to legally evict them without you receiving any rent payments.

I'm not saying you shouldn't become a landlord.

I'm saying if it happens, you need to have the money to pay the mortgage (if you have a mortgage) until you get them out and replace them with someone who will pay the rent.

It helps if you get first and last month's rent plus security deposit.

That's a lot money up front for a renter to pay.

Stories

I put closed after each closing, because I heard a few stories where at the closing table they didn't close. One was where one of the buyers was on the golf course. I almost had one. We closed in different rooms.

Once I heard a story where the contractor pushed the trash in the backfill against the foundation. I do not know if this is a true story. You want to be able to trust your contractor (s).

FALL 1994	GRADE-TYPE	GRADE	ATT.HRS	QUAL PTS
CON -151-001 CONSTRUCTION PROCESS		A	4.00	16.00

TOTAL	EHRS	GHRS	QPTS	GPA
CUR	4.00	4.00	16.00	4.000
CUM	4.00	4.00	16.00	4.000

CHAPTER EIGHTEEN

I Rent A Commercial Space

I've been a photographer since 1974. When I retired from construction (my real job other than investing), I wanted to start a photography business. I found what I thought was a good location. It was in an older building. I painted the walls in my unit and because the door into my unit was an old solid brown door, I had a custom door made of birch wood with glass to replace it.

As it turned out, it wasn't a good location. You can pay for a high traffic area where people will see your business as they drive or walk by or a less trafficked area, which should cost less, but then you need to put the money you saved from high rent into advertising to bring the people in.

My business didn't work, so I closed.

I also took my $800.00 custom door down and replaced it with the original door. It was heavy so I paid to have someone help me take it down and load it in my truck. Management remembered my custom door and told me they would sue me if I didn't replace it. There was a clause in my contract that stated any improvements stayed when tenant moves out. I had to pay again for help to load it in my truck and reinstall it.

Years later the building was torn down and my $800.00 door probably wasn't saved.

Morale of this story: read all contracts thoroughly before spending any money on improvements.

About the Author

This is my second book. I had thought about doing a class at our jr. college to share my stories, but decided to write this book instead.

I read a long time ago you won't get rich and become a millionaire by just working hourly. This is what got me interested in Real Estate Investing.

My first book is titled "Mom's Journey" about my Mom's music career and me personally selling her guitar to Vince Gill.

My third book will be on treasure hunting or drug running in the 1970s or a combination.

Currently working on getting an account on Etsy to market my photo collection from 1974.

I live in Littleton, CO with my wife Barbara and our dog Tracker.